ENOUGH!

How to Take Back Our Streets

ISBN: 9798683893736

Second Edition

Tom Monson Productions
409 North Pacific Coast Hwy., Suite 433
Redondo Beach, CA 90277
(541) 210-6698
Fax: (310) 1-772-8239

www.TomMonsonProductions.com

Dedication

This book is dedicated to three groups of people:

1. All my friends in law enforcement who put their lives on the line every day to protect and defend their fellow citizens,

2. All my friends who work tirelessly with law enforcement to keep their communities safer places to live and work, and

3. The people who's lives have been lost or who have lost their children, parents, and loved ones due to brutal crimes and other disasters.

You all have shown us how.

Forward

"In crime-ridden suburbs, sirens wail 24 hours a day. Vicious criminal gangs control neighborhoods where even the police are afraid to go.

"The War on Drugs has failed. Crack vials and needles dripping HIV-positive blood litter the city's streets, sidewalks, playgrounds and schoolyards.

"Uzis and Glocks, weapons once thought to be strictly military fare, have replaced Saturday night specials. Killings are commonplace.

"To protect their lucrative drug territories, gangs kill innocent people who unknowingly walk or drive at the wrong time through the wrong neighborhood. They call it 'going to Mayberry' when they describe their movement into communities where crime was never a problem before."

These grim predictions were written 25 years ago by Bill Bonner, President of the investment newsletter, Taipan.

Is This Really Our Future?

Mr. Bonner wasn't talking about poor, inner-city neighborhoods; he was talking about formerly-nice suburbs and small towns turned into crime-ridden ghettos — once beautiful neighborhoods taken over by gangs and drug-dealers.

Think about Long Island that was taken over by MS 13 and the terror that became commonplace and the killings of our children, rapes of our daughters, and the drugs that destroyed our treasure.

What Can We Do About It?

When faced with this realty, the common reaction is, "I'm only one person, what can I do about it?"

Is there something one person, or one family, can do about crime in our communities?

In this book, I will answer that question and prove to you that it is possible for one person to make a difference.

There is only one reasonable solution to reducing crime in our foreseeable future. And surprisingly, it isn't that hard, take much time, or put anyone in harm's way.

It's Not Hopeless!

I'm really concerned about what kind of a world we are leaving behind for our children. Crime, violence, and other social ills are not only destroying the American Dream, but with it, our children's future.

I believe that these issues can be positively addressed. I believe that we can make a difference and curb the rising tide of crime and violence.

I know it is not hopeless and if I present my case correctly, you will share this belief with me.

A Word of Caution

Of course, you know that just reading a book isn't going to change anything. Reading this book will help you understand the problem, maybe you'll even be able to intelligently discuss the problem, and explain what the solution has to be. If you are a politician, you'll have an in depth knowledge about crime issues, causes, and what to do about it. But none of that will fix anything.

The only thing that will bring about positive change is you, yes you, taking action.

It's all About the Possibilities

Across the land of the free, people are held hostage in the grip of fear. Afraid to leave their homes, apprehensive of the potential dangers, citizens give up their right to come and go as they please. They hand over the possession of their communities to thugs, violent gangs, anarchists, or criminal marauders who bring death and destruction to once a once peaceful place. They mistakenly expect the police to make their communities safe without their involvement or help.

The Purpose of this Book

One of the things that I will show you is the possibility of a better life for all of us. The hope that waits for our society is in the hands of the individuals who are willing to create a better community.

Our Children Are at Risk

There isn't one of us that wouldn't rescue a child in distress, but every day there are thousands of children who are destined to become criminals, drug addicts, alcoholics, or God help us are shot down in our streets. They are dropping out of school, ending up in hopeless situations, in prison, or dead.

But What Can I Do About It?

After reading this book, if you decide to do nothing else, then make your own dent in the problem and invest a little of your time and get involved with children.

Reach out and let these kids know that they have worth and that they can achieve something, if they have some direction. Join the Big Brother or Sister program, get involved in scouting, 4H, or FFA Youth Centers. If there is no youth center in your town, start one. If you don't do something, then who will?

INTRODUCTION

Why Me?

In 1988, I was sitting in my living room with my eight-year old daughter, watching a show about horses.

A news commentator broke in, "Eight year old girl shot while sitting in her living room with her father watching television."

It was a surreal moment. I glanced at my daughter. Wide eyed, she looked and I could see she was scared.

"Don't worry honey," I reassured her. "That was far far away. Nothing like that ever happens here. We are safe."

I lied. A few weeks before that a young girl was taken off a bike path, raped and murdered. I knew better.

A few days later, I was talking to my brother in law about it. He told me he heard the story and announced that he was moving to France because their laws were tougher and they didn't have this kind of problem.

At the time I was the executive director for the Small Business Advancement Institute. We produced videos, educational material, and training classes to help small business owners grow their businesses. It was a rewarding experience and there were a lot of business owners who needed help.

Later that year, a young man came to me and wanted me to help him produce a loss prevention video series about business crime. It made a lot of sense so we started working in loss prevention, and soon we were distributing programs throughout the United States.

In 1989 I decided to write a book that would show people, namely crime prevention officers, how they could set up a Community Watch Program.

When we first started compiling the information about the Community Watch System, I didn't realize the potential this program has to keeping communities safe. Like most people, all I knew was what I read in the newspapers, or had seen on television.

As part of the research team, I started talking to law enforcement and other people involved in the various programs.

It really hit me when I talked to Green County Missouri's Sheriff John Pierpont. Not only was he reducing crime, but he was also reducing the fear of crime, making communities more livable. I also realized that these towns and communities were gaining something else — a sense of community.

As we continued to develop the Community Watch, I kept hearing how the communities had become better places, neighbors getting to know neighbors again. It didn't take long before I too believed in the possibility that this single program would go a long way to making our streets safe by reducing crime.

As we continued to gather information, I could see that not only would reductions in crime be possible, the communities would gain the sense of pride and fellowship, but it had other possibilities.

I heard about disaster preparedness programs, the concept of community-involved policing, drug education, conflict resolution, school safety and so much more.

The thing that impressed me the most was the fact that the fear of crime was also reduced. I finally realize the main reason for the reduction in fear was caused by one thing — the knowledge we are doing something about it. We would no longer feel helpless, subject to the whims of the criminals who would take what we worked so hard for, and our cherish children.

There were three of us working to finish the manual. As we continued to compile the information into a usable form, we discovered that we needed to add examples of forms, booklets, and training devices. It seemed that every time we completed one of these tasks, there were two more we would have to add. We had law enforcement agencies from around the country sending us information and the tools they had developed.

There were about 30 crime prevention officers, public information officers, volunteers all pitching in to put this together. It was a very ambitious effort. Fortunately for us we were selling videos to pay all the expenses involved.

The project of building this manual had become a task of creating an entire community-wide, action-plan and watch system. We soon realized the manual alone wouldn't be enough. People wanting to take their streets back would need more than just a how-to book.

As we discovered, not only would we have to create the blueprint for the foundation, we would have to develop most of the tools to help people join with law enforcement to work together to make their community a better place to be.

I remember one meeting we had at a Holiday Inn, in Wilsonville, Oregon. There were 10 or 12 of us sitting around this huge table discussing what had to go into the manual. We were already over 500 pages, when Hank Salmons, a former chief of police said we needed something to deal with motivation. Because, he said too many programs fail within a couple of years because it eliminated the problem it was formed to solve. So we added the section on motivation.

This book is packed full of information about crime, crime prevention, and the latest thoughts about how to make our towns and cities safer places for us, our children, and our older folks.

The contents of this book comes from many others who took the time to help. Many of these people are the same ones who regularly put their lives on the line to make our streets safe. Others are the ones constantly working in different ways to achieve the same goal — a better place for us all.

Chapter 1

The Beginning of Hope — A Life Saved

"Get in the truck!" the man said gruffly as he pointed a gun at the twelve-year-old girl on her way home from school. With heart pounding, the young girl took several steps toward the man's truck then stopped, apparently having trouble breathing.

When the gunman dropped his guard, the girl ran as fast as she could for help. As she turned a corner, she saw a man snow-blowing a sidewalk. She ran to him and told what happened. The man called the police.

Rather than panicking and giving in to the man, this young girl knew what to do. Earlier that year, she had attended a Community Watch meeting in which a police officer explained what to do, what to pay attention to, and how to protect other potential victims.

When the police arrived, the young girl and another eye witness were able to give an accurate description of the potential molester and his vehicle.

Based on the descriptions, later that night the police arrested the man who tried to kidnap the girl. Further investigation linked the individual to the abduction and murder of another child three years earlier. He was later investigated in connection with several other disappearances in the area.

By her and the neighbor's actions, potential murders were prevented.

A Life Lost

This story is contrasted to the tragic killing of Polly Klaas in Petaluma, California. Polly was a twelve-year-old girl who was abducted from her bedroom at knife point. She was just one of the thousands of victims of these terrible crimes against our children — against us as a society.

The real tragedy of the Polly Klaas story is that her death could have been prevented once — possibly twice. A neighbor saw the murderer in the rear of her home, peeking in the window and did nothing about it — at least ten minutes before Poly was taken. Then, approximately two hours after the abduction, and she was reportedly still alive, the police questioned the convicted murderer and let him go.

As you can see, Polly's death could have been prevented. It is particularly disheartening when terrible crimes like this could have been prevented with nothing more than a phone call or even going out in the yard and questioning a prowler. It would cost nothing a very small commitment of time to reduce crime in most of our cities.

The trade off would be taking a few hours per year to train people about crime prevention with an end result of an increase in the quality of our lives and our freedom from fear and intimidation.

Community Watch Case Studies

In recent years, while our country's crime was skyrocketing, there were some communities enjoying substantial reductions in crime. These had been places where law-abiding citizens had once been afraid to walk down the street because the fear of crime gripped their lives. They have now become peaceful places where everyday people are able to pursue their interests without the fear of becoming victims of a violent crime.

Green County, MO

From 1981 to 1991, while the crime rate was dramatically climbing in surrounding areas, Green County, Missouri, enjoyed a fifty percent decrease in all types of crime. In fact, home burglaries decreased by eighty percent. Why? Sheriff John T. Pierpont understood the true concept of how the right kind of police work would have the net effect of making his community a safer place to live.

Seattle, WA

Even though Seattle recently has had its challenges, it hasn't always been that way. In 1972, Seattle participated in a crime prevention pilot project. The project brought the police and the citizens together with the common goal of reducing crime and improving Seattle's quality of life.

The project involved appointing police officers with the express duties of developing crime prevention programs. They were given four basic guidelines:

1. Create a dialogue between the citizens and the police.

2. Teach the people how to protect themselves.

3. Develop an effective communications system.

4. Report all suspicious activities to the police.

Since there was little in the way of how-to information available, Seattle had to develop its own strategies, materials, administration, communications and support system. It took several years but the program (mostly developed through trial and error) had the net effect of making Seattle a better place to live and work. In fact, when rated among all other big cities, until just recently, Seattle was rated as one of the most livable cities in the United States.

Detroit, MI

For over twenty years there were numerous examples of people in communities working to eliminate crime and the concept has been working well. Here is another:

Close to the same time, Detroit's chief of police was waging an all-out war on crime by establishing a special reactive task force to respond to robberies occurring in the city. This task force did little to reduce the crime rate and ended up alienating the department from the community.

In contrast, in 1976, William Hart was appointed chief and shortly after his appointment he implemented an experimental program in the Crary/St. Mary's district of the city. From 1977 to 1979 crime decreased in the district by 51 - 62 % (depending on the type of crime).

And even more impressive was that the following year an analysis was conducted on successful burglaries in the same district. Out of the homes that were burglarized, not one of them was one that participated in the program.

Why Isn't It Everywhere?

With so many successful programs out there, a reasonable question would be, "Why isn't Community Watch everywhere?"

The question I asked "If these programs work so well, why isn't everyone using them; why do we continue to hear stories every day about the crime and violence all around our country; why is it getting worse?"

Whether it is true or not, it seems that our nation's towns and cities are falling into the hands of hoodlums and criminals. These individuals are willing to rape, murder, steal, and commit violent crimes against anyone unfortunate enough to either get in their way or who has something they want.

With today's mobilization, criminals wander the highways expanding their misadventure to communities of all sizes. It is common knowledge that gangs are spreading their terror-ridden activities through a system of franchising. And, I don't need to tell you that on a national basis, sexual and violent crimes against children continue to rise.

We all face a real threat. How can we prepare ourselves for what is to come? I'll answer this question in this book.

Yet the crime rate grows

See for yourself. All you have to do is pick up a your computer, look at a newspaper, tune in your radio, or watch the television news, from anywhere in the United States, and you can see for yourself.

In our society today crime is the number one concern of our citizens. Studies conducted by the FBI, Department of Justice, and the media, all point to the growing concern about our personal safety and the financial devastation caused by crime. These studies also point out that there is a concern, not only about today, but also the future.

Where will the coming years will take our besieged cities and towns? In a recent article in the <u>Wall Street Journal</u>, it was illustrated that crime is the number one concern with eighty percent of the population. <u>USA Today</u> said that forty percent of us are changing our shopping habits because of the fear of crime; one out of four of us feels unsafe at shopping malls, and one out of three of us doesn't shop where we want to because of fear of violence.

Chapter 2

We Forget What They Steal

What these criminals steal are the life savings of the elderly, the profits born of the sweat and toil of business owners, and the lives, liberties, and the happiness of all of us.

There are numerous government and private agencies and organizations dedicated to working with crime victims. It's good to want to help, but the time to really help is before they become victims.

When you lose a child, nothing anyone can say or do will help. I can only speak for myself, but when my son was killed by a drunk driver, I had to come to terms with this tragedy on my own. No one could have done anything for me to make things right. After the fact, the time to make a real difference has already gone for the victims of crimes that have already been committed. The only meaningful difference would have been to prevent the crime from happening.

If someone steals the life savings of a senior citizen, we can give the money back and maybe reduce the threat of a financial catastrophe, but we can never take away the violation of having a criminal steal their life's savings.

An insurance payment will not replace a young man's passion for his car. It can't put back the pride of ownership he felt on those Saturdays when he would wash and carefully wax the representation of his diligence to save and keep his credit worthiness — so he could own his dream — only to have someone take it away to get a few dollars to buy some drugs or something else that would disappear.

Paying medical bills or offering some other worthless compensation will never — never, remove a rape victim's trauma and violation. Nothing will fix the fear and scars that will last forever in a changed life.

Where Are We Headed?

I ask questions like: Where is our country going? What kind of a future are we giving our children and our grandchildren?

When I was a kid, I remember being able to ramble freely around town. I knew my parents didn't have to worry about me getting into trouble, because outside of meeting the occasional bully or derelict, there wasn't much that could happen to me. If I made a mistake or did something stupid, it wasn't a big deal.

When I was young, if I looked at someone wrong, I could have been hit or beaten up or told that my mother wore army boots, but today such a mistake can be fatal.

But today, as parents we have more to worry about. Even simple mistakes can be deadly to our children.

Will we have to become a police state, with a police officer on every corner to insure our safety? If the current trends continue, this is a definite possibility. Are we willing to continue to pour billions of dollars into an ineffective method of trying to provide ourselves a safe place to work and live?

Or, are we willing to become a society, where criminals freely roam the streets searching for prey who are the fearful souls forced by necessity to venture out after dark?

Held Hostage

Daylight used to protect us but now the constant erosion of our safety and security is forcing us to stay inside all the time. Just look around and see the number of homes with security bars on the windows, alarm systems, and intruder-proof locks.

Today, more so than any time in our past, there are increased numbers of people wanting answers to this runaway problem — demanding more serious penalties for criminals, more police and more guns and self-defense devices.

Until we get a real handle on the problem, we can only expect more of the same?

What is the Real Problem?

Before we can identify a cure — if there is one, we must first identify the problem.

Crimes are committed for three basic reasons, motive, opportunity, and means.

Motives will always be here, greed, pleasure, perversion, or whatever. In a society where there are few or no deterrents, motives have fewer barriers and committing crimes become easier.

Since most crimes are opportunity driven, when targets are soft or open, criminals just help themselves. When there are fewer opportunities, there is less crime.

Means is the ability to commit the crime. It could be the available tools or a certain knowledge the criminal has that allows him to commit crimes. Historically, prisons have been a training ground for criminals to learn how to more efficiently commit crimes.

Left alone, the problem of crime and violence won't go away by itself.

People used to use the analogy of a cold. Meaning, if you have a cold, you can rest, take cold medicine, and in three to five days, the cold will probably go away. Or you could do nothing and the cold will probably go away in from three to five days.

Our crime problem isn't like a cold. It is more like cancer — eating away at the quality of our lives. If we do nothing, it will not go away — it will only get worse and consume us.

Chapter 3

Not long ago I read a survey in the *Wall Street Journal* that said forty percent of people have changed their way of life because of crime. Another survey indicated that seventy-seven percent of us live in the fear that we will become a victim of a violent crime. In response to that fear, seventy percent support tougher sentencing for criminals and a similar number want more prisons (twenty-one percent of federal prisoners were found guilty of low-level, non-violent crimes — such as possession of small amounts of drugs — but are serving lengthy sentences under mandatory minimums set by Congress.)

The logical response is to want to let non-violent offenders out of the prison system to make room for violent offenders. Since the number of violent crimes and individuals willing to commit them continues to rise, even this response may only provide a short-term solution to a greater problem.

Have You Had Enough Yet?

Most people sound an emphatic "YES!!!" to this question. People are fed up with crime and violence. They finally realize they are the ones being held hostage in their homes and apartments.

People are afraid to go out at night. Fear of rape, murder, assaults and robberies is keeping people inside their homes and they are getting tired of it.

I could write volumes about the problem. I could tell you stories about victims, cite statistics about rapes, sexual assaults, kidnapping, shootings, murders, gang violence, robberies, burglaries, auto theft, carjacking, child molestation, and the decay of our society, but you don't need me for that. You know what the problem is. That's why you're still reading. Right?

The New Cold War

The Wall Street Journal Called it The New Cold War. But it isn't a cold war; it's a hot war. Look at the death and destruction. Hundreds of people every week are shot in our big cities.

Searching for solutions, whole towns are arming themselves. People are ready to form vigilante groups and work outside the law to bring justice to suspected violators (forgetting about due process and what our system of justice is supposed to be, what it has to be.)

Most people, in an effort to stay alive, are just staying home, but even that isn't enough. Our children are being shot in their living rooms, bedrooms, parks, back seats of cars, at funerals, stores, and many other places

Is It Too Late?

There are many places we have already lost. Think about it. Are there places you wouldn't go because of the potential danger? Some of these places — and you know where I'm talking about — even the police won't go because they know that they are outgunned and outnumbered.

There are safer places in Iran, Iraq, or Afghanistan. To me, this just proves we have lost part of our country and some of our once great cities.

And like a cancer, it is coming to a town near you.

There are those who would argue that those places were never places where you could go in safety. That's nonsense because you can look at the numbers: crime and violence is more than just a serious problem; it is a real threat to our losing our life as we know it.

Is Our Personal Freedom at Stake?

A few years ago, the mayor in Washington, DC asked for the national guard to be deployed. This year, the mayor told them to stay away. In fact many mayors across the United States are telling the government to stay away. I'm wondering if that is in the best interests of the good people of their cities or if it is political. (This, once again, reinforces the idea that community safety and security shouldn't depend on the direction of political winds.)

Years ago, Senator Bill Bradley proposed the police should have the right to frisk anyone they suspect has a gun. Now that's considered unconstitutional by some.

After Rudy Giuliani solved the biggest part of New York's crime problem, subsequent politicians let it slide back into the crime-ridden city of olden days. Giuliani proved it could be done, but De Blasio proved that in order for you to keep a community safe it takes a commitment to continue programs that work and he also proves that a Community Watch program needs to be insulated from politics.

These are examples of how politicians can affect our safety and security because of political leanings and ineptitudes.

But at what expense? If we give up our rights as citizens to HOPE that our elected officials do the right thing for us to live in safely — provide safe places for our families — then we are screwed!

If you are willing to give up your rights as a citizen, then you will get whatever the winds of politics may blow your way. Maybe we should have to earn the right to be citizens.

As a generation, most of us have had it pretty easy. We haven't had to do much to be a citizen. Or at least some of us have not. How many of us vote on a regular basis? Are we just going along for the ride? Are we just taking what comes and getting involved only when absolutely necessary?

I'm sure many of you may not like reading this, but the truth is, we have allowed ourselves to get into this mess and if we are going to win the war on crime and violence, we are going to have to get involved. We are going to have to take an active role in our own defense to make our streets safe again.

How Big Is This Problem?

The following example illustrates the statistics on the effect of crime on you, your neighbors and your families:

Imagine yourself in a room with ninety-nine other people and ask, "If you have been a victim of a crime within the past two years, please rise." Sixteen people stand. Then say, "Please stand if any member of your immediate family has been a crime victim within the last two years." Eighty more people stand. Out of the hundred, ninety-six people have had their lives altered by crime and violence. Every person standing shares the emotional scars of a violation of his or her person or property.

Crime Statistics

Before I talk about crime statistics, I have to say that statistics are numbers. Crime victims are people, not nameless numbers, people whose lives have been changed or lost forever.

I wrote this in 1994. The numbers are different, but the principles are the same.

"Recent FBI statistics show that the crime rate has gone down by three percent. We all have heard about it and it should make us feel better, right?

"Maybe it makes you feel better, but not me. I'll tell you why:

"1. Over the past few decades, the crime rate has increased so much that a mere three percent reduction doesn't even come close to making our streets safe again.

"2. Today, so many crimes go unreported that we are not really seeing a true picture.

"3. And you can't tell me that shootings, muggings and rapes are going down.

"4. You can't tell me that crime in the schools is going down.

"5. And, in 1970 the odds of a woman being sexually assaulted in her lifetime were one in five; in the 80's odds had increased to one in four and right now the odds are that one in three women have the chance of being sexually assaulted during her lifetime. Think about it! Of every three women you know and love one of them will be sexually assaulted. Disgusting!

"So, as far as I'm concerned, this reported three percent reduction in crime doesn't even come close to the real figures. Even if it is accurate, such a reduction is nowhere near enough.

"I could talk to you all day about how crime affects our lives, how we are losing the quality of our lives, how much it costs us in taxes, how we worry about our children, and the quality of their lives. But you know all that.

"Maybe you have had enough and right now you are looking for an answer. I've got the answer. It is one that has worked in areas across the country and one that will work here.

"But before I tell you about it, you need to know the history of the problem and why it has gotten this bad."

Identifying the Problem

The real problem is fear. People are afraid to go out at night, to have their children go to school. They fear that someone will steal their dreams, the fruit of their work or what they hold most precious.

EMERSON SAID: "Fear defeats more people than any other thing in the world."

Why? Because fear causes wasted energy, avoidance, or inaction. People react either in fighting - taking the law into their own hands, flight - they run away, or freeze and do nothing.

While it is true that fear strikes at the individual core of liberty, fear and inaction causes us to die a thousand deaths.

I talk to police officers all the time who tell me that the average citizen doesn't care about what is going on as long as it doesn't affect them. I believe people care for two reasons: first, I think people would do something if they knew what to do; second, I think the inaction on the part of a lot of people is caused by fear.

People living next to a levee that is threatened by rising flood water, know what they have to do — reinforce the levee. They are afraid that the levee may burst and they stand a chance of being swept away; nonetheless, they keep on filling, and stacking sandbags. Why? Because they know what has to be done and how to do it.

How Did It Get So Bad?

It has taken years to get to the point where we are today. There is no quick fix to make this problem go away. If we are to take back our lost communities, we are going to have to take them back street by street, neighborhood by neighborhood.

What Is the Cause?

To find the real cure, we have to examine the root cause. Years have been spent on researching questions like:

Is it because of a decline in morals — caused by the decline of the nuclear family?

Did it start with the banning of prayer in school?

Is it because more moms are working outside the home?

Is it because of media publicity given to crime?

There are many more probabilities for the root cause of crime. But until mankind understands how the brain can be altered to cause a conformity of behavior, we will need to deal with crime and criminals in real terms.

You can't change human nature. Many people are honest because they choose to be honest. Some people are honest because they have not had an opportunity to be dishonest. Study after study illustrates that if given the opportunity, a lot of people would commit a crime to gain materially, if they felt they could get away with it.

Again I could spend years researching the root causes and spend years providing solutions that you may or may not agree with, but that will not help us understand what we have to do to make our streets safe again.

Let's look at what we have been doing and some reasons why it has not been working.

Why Isn't Law Enforcement Isn't working?

In many areas, current methods of law enforcement are not working to protect the average citizen. Over the past 20 to 30 years, there have been dramatic increases in crimes of violence, crimes relating to business, and crimes directed at our youth.

Most law enforcement administrators readily admit that robberies, assaults and various other crimes continue to rise (not only in numbers of offenses but also in the level of violence of these offenses).

We all pay, not only in the quality of life, but with our checkbooks. As I mentioned, odds of woman being sexually assaulted has increased dramatically, but did you know that during the same period that the cost to American business for shoplifting and employee theft increased to more than one hundred billion dollars. Guess who pays the tab?

Is it the Government's Fault?

If you're like most people, you blame the government, namely the police. If you were to point your finger at the guilty party to fix blame, and you turned your hand over, you would see more fingers are pointing in your direction than in the direction of who you want to blame.

It's not the police or the government's fault. It's our fault. We all have to share the blame for our crime problem. The answer comes from Sir Robert Peel, who established the London Metropolitan Police when he wrote the mission statement for law enforcement and created a model for crime-free communities. Here is what he said as he addressed law enforcement:

"To maintain at all times a relationship with the public that gives reality to the historic tradition that the police are the public and that the public are the police: the police being only the members of the public that are paid to give full-time attention to duties which are incumbent on every citizen in the interest of community welfare and existence."

What Sir Robert Peel said was that <u>we are all in this together</u> and that it is everyone's responsibility to police our communities.

Possibly part of our problem is we believe the mission of law enforcement is enforcing the law. That implies their primary mission is to make the laws work — give them teeth, and put the bad guys behind bars.

Unfortunately, we will always need people willing to kick in a door, not knowing what's on the other side. We will always need people with courage, willing to put themselves in harm's way.

The mission statement for police should be dictated by their bosses, the people who pay them. When Robert Peel wrote the mission statement, he said two things that need to be applied to our situation today.

1. The primary duty of the police is to prevent crime.

2. We all share responsibility to insure our own safety.

We are all in this together. The police have to empower people to take responsibility for their own safety; otherwise, they are enabling people to become victims.

We all have to own this. If we don't, then someone else will and rule our lives. It's that simple.

Over 20 years ago, in a letter to officers of a the Chicago Police Department, the superintendent wrote, "As modern urban life becomes more challenging and complex, so does the role of police officers, who must be even more creative and ingenious. We must constantly seek out new ways for citizens and their government to work in partnership toward solving the range of difficult and constantly changing problems that still confront us."

Work in partnership? You mean like the police are the public and the public must take ownership of the police?

In a general order issued in April of 1989, a memo from the Colorado Springs Police Department is quoted, "When police agencies permit themselves to become entirely reactive, they see their responsibilities as simply to pick up the pieces after something has gone wrong; by preventing crime, police agencies across the country have created new roles for themselves as positive forces for social betterment."

Wasted Energy

More often than not, there is a lack of inter-agency cooperation between many law enforcement agencies located in or near the same jurisdiction. The level of cooperation between related agencies varies from state to state. Politics and responsibilities often get in the way of the primary mission of law enforcement. Duplication of efforts, joint action plans, lack of sharing knowledge, training, and materials are a few of the considerations that impede the process.

Agencies such as the city police, the county sheriff, state police, federal law enforcement agencies, and the criminal justice system including juvenile, parole, probation, and corrections departments, all work independently, often out of sync, trying to achieve different goals for the same community. What they should be working toward are priorities and how they fit into the needs of the communities.

Some people tell me that the police are only interested in protecting their own, the thin blue line, the brotherhood as they used to call it. I have talked to police who feel that their job is to "hook 'em and book 'em, then get the hell out of there." On the other hand, there are a vast number of police officers who work very hard to protect the people and keep the streets safe.

In my opinion, the biggest failing of the police is not providing the necessary leadership to teach people how to prevent crime and improve the quality of life in the community. Simple things like home security surveys, personal safety classes, informing folks about fraud and scams directed at them, what is and how to report suspicious activity, and myriad other things could go a long way to reducing crime and improving the livability of our communities.

Apathy

I talk to law enforcement and crime prevention people every day and many of them believe that everyday people are apathetic. Some of them tell me that people are only interested in their own circumstances.

But when I talk with average folks, they feel powerless to protect themselves and their families. It's not that they are apathetic — they do care — they would do something, if they knew what to do.

What may appear as apathy is really just not knowing what to do or how to do it. If the folks knew what to do, they would do it. I guarantee it.

People Make All the Difference

If you are like most of the people I talk to, you may be asking yourself what can one person do to make a difference? People working individually can and do make a difference all the time, when they know what to do. In many cases, when there is a need for action, and the action required is apparent, people figure it out, and take action. You see a house on fire, you run to see if anyone is in the house and get them out. It happens every day.

Here are a few more examples:

The Church Hill neighborhood in Richmond, Virginia, experienced three murders, two rapes, and one hundred thirty-four burglaries in one year. One resident decided enough was enough. She organized the Church Hill Crime Watch, combining Neighborhood Watch basics with a neighbor-to-neighbor telephone network and a monthly newsletter to spur action and sustain communication. The program flourished. Two years later: no murders, no rapes, and only twenty burglaries.

A Detroit, Michigan, woman channeled her grief into action, after her son was shot to death in a dispute. She created Save Our Sons and Daughters (SOSAD), a violence prevention and grief support group that already has chapters in two other cities. SOSAD focused attention on anti-violence education for parents and children, on positive activities for youth, and on helping those who have lost a loved one to violence, cope effectively with their grief.

A Ypsilanti, Michigan, woman decided that she had to do something when she found out that drug dealers were hiding drugs in her bushes. By going door-to-door in the neighborhood, she found other families worried about the violence, school dropout rates, and youths' low self-esteem that contributed to the drug problem. The group set out to create positive alternatives to drugs and crime that, with persistence, not only drove drug dealers away, but won the enthusiastic support of the youth.

These instances and many more like them, prove to me that people are not apathetic; they just need leadership and direction.

Chapter 4

Deterrents

Violations of our rights occur because criminals don't feel society's deterrents are sufficient to prevent them from committing crimes. In other words, they feel that the chances of getting caught and/or punished are low and what they have to gain (by committing their crime) is worth the potential risk.

Today, there are many places in the United States where they will not even prosecute criminals for certain crimes and other crimes they do not hold them at all. New York has a zero dollar bail. You commit a crime, the police arrest you, take you downtown, take your picture, and you go home, or as it turns out you go out and rape, steal, or burglarize someone's home to celebrate.

Other places like San Francisco you can shoplift or steal items that are worth less than $1,000 and not be prosecuted for it. Many drug addicts pay for their drugs with profits from shoplifting. So these laws compound other problems. But who do you suppose pays for the losses business suffer due to shoplifting? We all do!

Whether it's true or not, the chance of getting caught or prosecuted today doesn't appear to be too great and it seems that nobody cares. Muggings, and abductions often remain unsolved because they are committed in broad daylight with dozens of witnesses, who when asked, didn't see anything.

The Catherine Susan "Kitty" Genovese case comes to mind, where it was reported that 38 bystanders did nothing or shut their doors to silence her cries for help and her screams during the half hour her attacker stabbed her 14 times.

Study after study concurs that the number one fear for criminals is getting caught and going to prison. But today, they face little threat of getting caught (because of the tremendous workloads and defunding of the police) and even if they are caught, they know that the chance is even smaller that they will have to serve any serious time, let alone the full sentence.

Does the Media Add to the Prestige of Being a Criminal?

Everyone knows the names of Jeffrey Dahmer, Ted Bundy, John Wayne Gacy, and Charles Manson. These twisted individuals and other violators of human rights are often immortalized by an unwitting accomplice. Media narratives and visual representations of their exploits of robbery, rape, and murder reinforce the images of their twisted acts. But more important to them is the immortality they gain — even though it may be of infamy — only serve to fuel the antisocial desires of some of these hardcore criminals.

The ability to gain media coverage for crimes only elevates the offender's prestige and stature within the circle of criminals. When they descend into surroundings with other criminals, these individuals often boast of the media coverage they gained for their sordid exploits. If they end up behind bars, these criminals are often revered and glorified by their contemporaries and often they are followed by groupies.

What role do you see the media playing in the problems related to crime and the prevention of its escalation? The media has the potential to educate the public and could therefore be an important device to teach people about crime prevention. Unfortunately, in many cases they tend to serve their own interests by promoting the old saying, "If it bleeds, It leads," which supports the notion that they are in it for the money.

This has always been my biggest complaint about the media. Sure they will show you what is wrong with society, and will only show you a very small portion of what is right and rarely will they tell you how to prevent a crime from happening.

There was a time when the media felt their role was to act as a watch dog warning people about the police and exposing fraud and "bad" police practices. But that role has fallen to a permanent dogma that the "Police are the enemy." Tainting the public's view of the police which causes people to mistrust police and be afraid of them when they have an interaction with law enforcement.

I believe this is one of the reasons there is so much violence aimed at police today. Today more law enforcement officers are attacked than any other time in history. If you don't believe that, just look at the statistics.

Prison as a Deterrent

Most criminals are aware of the fact that if our criminal justice system sentences them to prison for a fixed term, it means they will actually only do a fraction of the time. Due to overcrowding and liberal judicial policies, criminals are often released when they have served only a very small part of their time.

Most people aren't aware of it, but every criminal knows the penal system plays by different rules than does our court system. Our penal system and criminal justice system are separate entities; therefore, what the jury, judge, and/or the prosecution order as punishment for their crimes, isn't necessarily what will be carried out. And, the criminals know that they won't have to serve as much time as the courts order.

If a court sentences a criminal to twenty years, he or she can get out much sooner for a number of reasons. In effect, when a court system passes judgment, it only serves as a recommendation of the length of time actually served.

Many people believe the system serves only to encourage criminals to be criminals.

Trade Schools for Criminals

Historically prison is a trade schools for criminals. Cons teach other cons about all the "new-and-improved" ways to take what others have worked so hard to gain. Techniques for committing burglaries, robberies, fraud, and numerous other crimes are passed on from one criminal to the next. Since they have a lot of time on their hands, this type of education is almost an expected form of behavior.

When criminals are released, they often go out within a few days and commit the very same crime for which they were originally incarcerated, but with added confidence from what they learned in prison. Their skills have been upgraded because other cons were able to teach them improved methods of stealth and efficiency. Their chances of getting away with their crime are increased because of what they learn in prison.

Should People Arm Themselves?

In an effort to gain safety and security, our citizens in record numbers are buying guns. Does this mean that more criminals will be shot? Possibly, but the real victims are going to be the children, friends, and families of the gun owners. Many more innocent lives will be taken because of accidental shootings than criminals being shot during the commissions of crimes.

Children playing with accessible, loaded guns will turn them on themselves, their friends, and their siblings in either a demonstration of power or some other unknowing act. Guns cause more accidental shootings, killing innocent people, then they prevent crimes.

Family members and friends will die in the middle of the night because a sleepy-eyed, fuzzy-minded household-defender may mistake them for some external threat and start shooting.

Other family members, with a tendency for domestic violence or abuse, will turn these guns on each other as either a defensive measure or in a fit of rage, and change what could have been a potentially correctable situation into a homicide.

An untrained person with a gun stands a good chance of losing the gun to an experience criminal during a confrontation and the gun is then turned on the defender. What may have been a robbery turns into a murder.

Guns also make a marketable piece of contraband for thieves to take during the commission of burglaries and robberies. Those stolen guns now go to other criminals and create more armed criminals, and put guns in the hands of would-be criminals.

Guns are not the answer. Untrained people with guns are unsafe, not only to themselves, but to everyone around them.

Tougher on Crime

Many People Believe that getting tougher on crime is the answer but to be rational about criminals is not to be soft on crime.

Violent criminals should indeed be punished harshly.

I recently suggested it would take a whole league of brave legislators to step up to the plate. But this doesn't seem to be a priority on their part.

Getting tough on criminals means making a punishment fit the crime. Only when a criminal knows that he or she will be prosecuted and serve the entire sentence, will punishment be an adequate deterrent.

We have witnessed the decay of our society, where crime is terrible and the best people can say is, "I hope it doesn't happen to me."

Is Community Policing the Answer?

The problem is most cops only see the worst people or people at their worst. So the community policing legislation did not do much to improve crime statistics. Until each of us has a personal escort of a police officer, we won't feel safe. But even then, we won't be able to afford it.

The idea is put 100,000 new police officers on the street, but within four or five years we will need 200,000 or even 300,000 more. There will be no end to it.

The fact was that we were already over 100,000 police officers short from what we needed to keep the streets safe, and it would never work because the crime rate kept rising.

I knew of communities where police spend their entire shift just going from one call to the next, falling farther behind. They just try to close the books on as many cases as they can. But the numbers of unsolved crimes continues to grow.

In some cases they reclassified different types of crime from felonies to misdealers just to cook the books and be able to say felonies dramatically dropped while the number of the same crimes increased.

So, you never know what is going on because the politicians in government and police agencies continue to tell us the truth as they intemperate it to make themselves look good. No one seems to be able to figure it out and I don't know if anyone is even trying to find the answer.

So the final thought about Community Policing is this, I've personally know a lot of cops over the years and many of them have felt the same way, being community orientated was always part of their way of doing business. Dave Baleria told me one time that his job was community orientated.

There are two types of policing, reactive or proactive. Coming from the reactive side means that when a crime happens, you respond to it to clean up the mess. Being proactive means you want to eliminate the crime before it happens.

Tony Robbins, the motivational speaker, said reactive is for losers and proactive is for winners.

The only way to be proactive is to participate with the townsfolk in keeping them and the town safe. It's not just the police's responsibility to do it, the responsibility rests on all of us.

Chapter 5

Who's Winning the War?

In a 1993 speech, Richard M. Daley, the mayor of Chicago said, "Community policing means reinventing the Chicago Police Department. It means doing more than responding to calls for service and solving crimes. It means transforming the Department to support a new, proactive approach to preventing crimes before they occur. It means forging new partnerships among residents, business owners, community leaders, the police, and City services to solve long-range community problems.

"As Mayor, I recognize that the police can't do it alone. If community policing means reinventing the way the Chicago Police Department works, it also means reinventing the way all city agencies, community members, and the police, work with each other. Everyone must share the responsibility for the safety and well-being of our neighborhoods."

It was a nice speech, but when political winds blew, so did the proposed changed and the idea was left behind for whatever reason. What this community needs to do is take ownership of the police, because in the real world, the good citizens of Chicago are the ones paying the police for their services.

In a similar time, if I recall correctly, the citizens of Dallas, Texas took ownership of the police and gave them what they needed to keep the city and the folks safe.

Solving crimes has been, and always will be, an essential part of law enforcement. But preventing crimes is the most effective way to create a safer environment for ourselves, our families, and our neighbors.

Our Choices

I know I've mentioned it before, but our only choices are fight, flight, or freeze and do Nothing. If you were to imagine yourself as a gazelle taking a lunch break on the Serengeti, and a hungry lioness came your way, you would have three options:

1. You could take flight—run away to a safer place,

2. You could fight—stand and protect yourself, or

3. You could freeze and do nothing and hope she would get interested in someone else.

Take Flight: For us humans it's a different story. As evidenced by the recent decade, movement of our population to the suburbs, to small towns and even to other countries shows that many people have chosen to run away from crime. But, as in the animal kingdom, predators follow prey. I met a guy who moved from Los Angeles because the meth problem was so bad. When he got to Oregon, he found the problem was even bigger than it was in LA. His next move was to move to Missouri where the problem was even bigger. He found out that almost every corner of our country, has been experiencing increases in all types of drug abuse which results in all types of crime.

Fight: Prey willing to fight back is less likely to be on the top of the predator's dining list. Since most criminals take the easiest route to commit their crimes, they are less likely to try to victimize someone who is ready, willing, and able to fight back.

Do Nothing: If you were one of the gazelles standing there, and a lioness were to approach, you wouldn't just stand there and hope that she wouldn't pick you for a meal. When threatened, even the least intelligent member of the animal kingdom knows he has to either fight or take flight. Yet, most people choose to do nothing about crime and they just hope they are not the ones eaten, if they even take the time to recognize the threat.

It just goes to show, that even the dumbest animal will do something when it is faced with a serious threat, whereas we smart humans seem to be the only members of the animal kingdom that will do nothing, and hope that crime will not affect us.

Wishful Thinking

It isn't just wishful thinking to expect to live in a community where every citizen has the right to life, liberty and the pursuit of happiness. Yet every year millions of Americans are robbed, raped, murdered, or become victims of crime.

What can make every town and city in our besieged country a safer and better place to be? Why does common sense elude us? How can we prevail and impart safe living to the citizens of our cities and towns? How can we create a plan to build safe communities?

Mobilize

If a foreign power lands on our shores and kills, rapes, and robs our people to the extent we are currently witnessing, you can bet that we would unite as a nation and take the necessary actions to stop it. As a united people, we would accept required sacrifices.

To eliminate the threat, we would gladly grow victory gardens, accept gas rationing, volunteer for civil defense, and go to work in factories to manufacture the goods necessary to beat our common foe. It would all seem so simple, because everyone would know what had to be done and we would be willing to do whatever was necessary to insure our way of life.

We have done it before, **why not now**?

Contributions of the Media

I used to believe that the media contributed to the problem, causing people to be hardened to the difficult situation.

But now I believe that the media is doing us a big favor, but they are not finishing the job.

The bad news the media reports makes us aware. It isn't their responsibility to make us care. It isn't their job to make us care about the victims. And I guess they don't feel it is their place to help us find solutions — and oh yes there are solutions — some good and some not so good.

The media helps us become aware of the problem. Otherwise, we wouldn't know something needed to be done about it.

Love It or Lose It

During the 1960's there was a popular saying directed at those who were not satisfied with the way things were in our country — people who objected to the Vietnam War, government policies, or conditions in the country, were told to "Love it or leave it."

Today a greater number of people are dissatisfied — tired of crime, violence, and deterioration of our cities — people who realize that we now face as big a threat to our freedom as our parents and grand-parents faced in the 30's and 40's. I tell you, people, you better love it or you are going to lose it.

I say, "Let's revive and revise the slogan of the 60's to read LOVE IT OR LOSE IT." And most of you will agree with me.

In the history of the world there has never been such a country where freedom has been the hallmark for so many millions of people. If the United States had not been here during the Second World War, what would the world be like now? We sit here thinking about what a wonderful addition to world history the U.S. has been and could be, but we are in a dangerous situation, and I believe we are facing a tipping point and stand a real threat of losing our country and the freedom and benefit we have taken for granted for so many years.

Traditional thinking dictates that we put more police on the street —every time we add more police we need even more and where will it end? A cop on every corner?

Chapter 6

Safe Communities

Will we find a way to permanently reduce crime in America or is that just the way it is?

How are we going to make our towns safe places for our children to grow up?

Almost fifty years ago, there were several communities that realized there was an ever-growing crime problem and they found a way to do something about it. In fact, there were dozens of small and large cities and counties that discovered effective ways to reduce crime.

They did something about crime, and in many of these areas today, crime is under control.

It started in individual neighborhoods, with people who wanted to reduce crimes in their communities and they took action. Soon they saw progress, and moved from neighborhoods to city-wide projects. It didn't take long for them to figure out that these programs would work in other areas, fighting other types of crime so they started expanding into other kinds of programs.

One of the key elements of these successful programs was that people wanted a change, they were willing to take responsibility for their own security, and took action.

A proactive approach to law enforcement, recently designated Community Policing, is demonstrated here because of the effect it has on the community.

But don't confuse Community Orientated Policing with

Community Watch.

Solving the Problem

I have already demonstrated there are many communities around our country where people are willing to take action; the problem is that until just recently, they did not know what to do.

More Examples of Winning

Here are a few of the places that saw significant reductions in crime:

- Bromley-Heath housing project in Boston, Massachusetts, robberies were reduced by 77%.

- Lakewood, Colorado, burglary was slashed by over 70%.

- Seattle, Washington, burglary was cut in half.

- Easton, Pennsylvania, reported crime fell by almost 30%.

- Minneapolis, Minnesota, residential burglaries decreased by over 20%.

These are all examples of places where the citizens accepted the responsibility of their own safety, and went to work with, instead of depending on, law enforcement to make their communities better places to live.

These places turned the dream of a safe community into reality where children can safely plan, people can stroll down the street and feel they will get where they're going safely.

So Many Failures

Why were there these success stories while so many other failed?

There is a reason why these towns, cities, and counties became safer places to live, and the formula for their success isn't a guarded secret. In fact, the techniques to curb the onslaught of criminal activity are known to most law enforcement agencies.

They don't implement them because they are either unwilling to accept the recipe for change, they don't believe they can really bring about change, they refuse to accept that there is really a problem with crime, or they use the excuse that they don't have the staff, power, or money to bring about change.

The First Step

The first step for a cure is recognizing the problem. I'm sure you know that lately there's been a lot of talk about community policing.

The reason: because we are finally recognizing that reactive law enforcement methods do not really work. They never have. You can't keep someone safe by making sure you get there after a crime has occurred — even if you get there quickly.

Rising crime and violence are real problems, not only to law enforcement, but a recent survey showed that crime and violence were the number one concerns of eight out of ten people.

What is the answer? Right now everyone is pointing to community policing. But is community policing really our best answer to combat the crime and violence in our country?

Possibly, if it's done right, it could be a big part of the answer. But there is one fundamental problem regarding community policing .

And that is...If you were to ask five people—what community policing is—you would probably get five different answers.

So it is important that we come up with, and agree on, a definition of what community policing really is.

Almost two hundred years ago, Sir Robert Peel, the father of modern day law enforcement, told us it was the responsibility of each citizen, to insure for our own safety—and that the police were also citizens who were paid to devote their full-time efforts to deal with crime and criminals. So just to be perfectly clear, what he said is, it's the responsibility of all of us — not just up to the police, to make our streets safe.

For our definition, the term community policing has one word missing and you know what it is. It is Community "involved" Policing. Because only when the citizens get involved in insuring for their own safety, can we turn the spiraling crime and violence rates around.

And if we can agree on this, then we can also agree that Community Watch is the only, best answer we have for keeping our streets safe.

Get Residents Involved

Now when I talk about people's involvement to help make their streets safer, I'm not talking about vigilantism or taking the law into your own hands... What I'm talking about is working with law enforcement, rather than depending on law enforcement for your safety.

Working Together

When an entire community is involved in policing, not only is the community a safer place, but police work is much more effective.

Here are a few goals to reach this better state of being:

1. Work together to fight crime and the fear of crime.

2. Educate the folks about things like disaster preparedness, health education, fire prevention, school safety, drug prevention, and anything else that concerns the police and the people.

3. And finally, to instill a greater sense of community. Put the neighbor back into the neighborhood.

What does law enforcement have to gain?

Just for starters, there will be numerous sets of eyes and ears reporting suspicious activities and when necessary, making themselves available to be reliable witnesses — which results in higher apprehension and conviction rates.

Second, law enforcement will save time and money, not only in setting up a community policing program, but the reduction in crime will put less of a demand on staff resources. Being able to quickly respond and apprehend suspects will cut time spent on investigations, so there will be more time available to spend on the really important cases.

Finally, when law enforcement works with the people of a community, it is a better place for everybody.

What Is Community Watch?

Community Watch is a community-wide action plan and system developed to combat crime and criminals with the coordinated efforts and elements of both the proactive and reactive sides of law enforcement. The system unites criminal justice organizations, businesses, governmental agencies, civic organizations, professional organizations, schools, neighborhood associations, and citizens at large in a common cause effort to make our communities a safer place in which to live, work, and raise a family.

The action plan calls for the identification of all the formal and informal resources and then mobilizes them into a coordinated effort. This effort becomes a force that directs its efforts to establishing goals that lead to the end result of creating a crime-free, safe community.

A Community Watch program is a win-win situation for everyone—everyone except criminals, gangs, drug dealers, and others who would do harm to community members.

It has taken years for our crime problem to get to current levels and it is going to take years to turn it around... however, it is possible. But it can only happen when we take responsibility for our own safety and security.

And it may not even take years. I've seen too many communities, where feelings of safety and trust are restored within months of the program starting.

A Message to the Police

Whatever you do will not work unless the people you serve not only buy into it — but more importantly, take ownership of it. Like it or not, it all belongs to us anyway.

We are all basically the same because we all share the same dreams for our children, but first and foremost, we are all town folk. What we do to make a living is only a consideration.

A Message to the Town Folk

This is your town; the police work for you, and you should make sure that you work with the police. You should become part of the police and always remember that the police are citizens first and that you pay them to deal with crime and their first responsibility is to prevent crime. That is the definition of "protect."

Community Watch Combines the Best of Two Worlds

First, it acknowledges and reinforces the value of deterrents offered by the criminal justice system. It increases the chances of offenders getting caught, frees up the investigative time of law enforcement, and it provides additional funding necessary to meet existing criminal justice needs.

Second, it mobilizes the vast information resource of ordinary people. People are able to provide valuable information to the police to make their efforts more effective and more rewarding.

Exposing law enforcement officers to positive interaction with ordinary people will allow them to see that most people are generally supportive of law enforcement. Since many officers are reacting to crimes, after they happen, they mostly see the negative side of human nature. This would balance their interaction with ordinary folks.

The Community Watch organization also becomes a resource for law enforcement. Instead of having dozens of witnesses who didn't see anything, police now can gain an accurate description of the criminal, his getaway car, and which way he went. Plus they can have the information quickly, without having to spend valuable time looking for a few cooperative witnesses.

Years of experience demonstrate that proactive crime prevention programs are proven to substantially reduce crime by removing the opportunity. Reductions in the various types of crime rates are reported to be anywhere from 10 to 70% and more.

Why We Need Community Watch

Over the past twenty-plus years, the crime rate has seen dramatic increases in both personal crimes of violence and crimes relating to business. Current methods are not working.

I have already shared with you what I believe may be in store for us during the next twenty years. Unless we unite and take action now, there will be no way to change this future. Sooner or later someone will have to do something - I think this is something we should do, instead of leaving it to our children and grandchildren to deal with.

Proactive and Reactive Programs

In simple terms, proactive programs are aimed at "before the fact," kinds of actions. Reactive programs are aimed at "during" or "after the fact" kinds of actions. When related to crime, proactive equals preventing crime. All other criminal justice programs are geared towards "during" or "after the fact" actions; thus, they are reactive in nature.

The truth is, aggressive proactive programs will enhance and enable reactive programs. Reactive efforts can feed valuable information to the proactive programs, thus serving to enable them.

The Community Watch program was developed for the whole community to participate. The plan, however, allows that one person or group of persons may apply the program without the entire community adopting it.

The Case for Community Policing

In an article for <u>THE POLICE CHIEF</u>, Chief Richard Overman of Delray Beach Police Department, Florida, talked about how the role of the police is changing, but he questioned the ability of some administrators to change with the times. He gives some advice for administrators,

"... this notion of changing the way we do business, setting our priorities and measuring success must be sold to — rather than forced on — our people.

If we are to be successful in taking back our streets, we must also be able to define our responsibilities as a police department. For the past quarter-century, we have been telling citizens that if they would lock their windows, put dead bolts on their doors and install alarm systems, we would take care of them. But while we thought we could take care of them, the truth is that we can't — and I'm not sure we ever could ... police officers work twenty-four hours a day, seven days a week, 365 days a year — and still can't be everything to everybody."

He continued to talk about how people must take responsibility for their own protection, and that it is the role of the police department to help the community get started.

He concluded, "They must take ownership and have a stake in the outcome in order to ensure success. What we know for sure is that to ignore the future is the worst alternative of all. Since that's where we're all headed, we must dedicate our maximum effort to affect it positively for our communities' sakes as well as our own. While it is not without risk, we—as leaders—must take the first step. The future depends on it."

Reducing Crime

Earlier, we talked about the real problem. A deeper discussion would reveal that anyone who knows anything about criminology will agree there are three main ingredients that make up a crime:

MOTIVE — The reason to commit the crime. The desire to gain materially, socially, or psychologically.

Trying to eliminate the motive for criminals to commit crimes is one of the great social questions of our time. Working with children to eliminate some of the driving forces that cause them to choose a life of crime, is something that we may have to work on for the next thousand years. However, it's been demonstrated that youth-oriented programs are having a positive effect on potential criminal behavior.

OPPORTUNITY — The chance to commit the crime. Be it an open door, an unlocked car, or a vulnerable potential victim.

For the most part people steal because it is easy. If you make it less easy, crime reductions will result. Let's say that there is a drug addict who has a fifty dollar a day habit and he supports the habit by burglarizing homes. About half of all burglaries occur through unlocked doors and windows, so if everyone were to lock up, the threat of being burglarized would be substantially reduced. Possibly a drug addict would be unable to take what he needs. He might wait until the next day, go to another town, or maybe he will try to get some help. In any event, this crime has been either slowed down or prevented.

TOOLS OR KNOWLEDGE — A gun for an armed robbery, a crowbar for a burglary, or the knowledge of how to take what someone has earned.

Tools will always be available. Unless we outlaw tools, knives, and guns, we have to accept the fact that the tools will always be with us. The knowledge to commit crimes is driven by the motivation.

If you take away the motivation you will take away the desire to gain the knowledge.

If you take away the opportunity and the motivation, there is a good possibility of a substantial reduction in crime.

Fighting to Reduce Crime

Community Watch utilizes programs to reduce the shear number of crimes by reducing the opportunity, and diverting the motivation. The reactive side of law enforcement maintains a stronger deterrent because they have gained a resource consisting of thousands of eyes and ears.

Law enforcement also becomes a resource to the Community Watch organization to help them reduce the opportunity and reduces the motivation to commit crime. Training and education become powerful weapons wielded by proactive law enforcement agencies.

Chapter 7

All-around the world, elements of Community Watch have been working effectively to not only reduce crime, but to make communities better places to live and work. It works because Community Watch utilizes tried and true methods of varied and successful programs to improve the quality of life when a community initiate the plan.

Elements of Community Watch

Community Watch unites related programs into a network headed either by an individual or committee who administrates and coordinates the efforts into a single program with a single agenda. Its sole purpose is making the community a better place in which to live and work. Elements can be utilized in an area-wide plan instead of duplicated efforts being made by various groups.

The foundation of Community Watch is effectively being used in large numbers of communities around the world and has been for centuries.

Neighborhood Watch

What is Community/Neighborhood Watch? The primary purpose of the Community Watch program is to improve the quality of live in the community. Most often, the motivation to start a program is to reduce crime and the possibility of crime.

Primarily, this program benefits people living in the participating areas of a community. (However, everyone benefits from reductions in crime because it improves the livability of the whole community.)

This program motivates and mobilizes individual neighbors to look out for each other. This program also teaches individuals and families how to safeguard themselves, as well as their homes from criminals and in the event of a disaster.

Successful programs include regular training, communication, and interaction integrated throughout the whole community. Phones and cameras are also used to record observed suspicious activities.

Other areas of concern can also be addressed by the organization. Things like health training, fire prevention, zoning or planning issues are commonly discussed in community meetings.

RESULTS: Reduction and prevention of home burglary, rape, murder, vandalism, drug offenses, auto theft, assaults, fraud, and con games. Other gains are disaster preparedness, health, safety, and civic planning issues.

Safe Streets

How Community Watch Groups Keep Their Streets Safe. Most of the time when police catch a criminal, it is because of direct involvement of a citizen. They receive a call describing something unusual or a crime in progress so they, the police, can act on it. Most often when they are able to apprehend a suspect it, is because of an accurate description given by someone who knew what to look for and how to report it.

Neighborhood Watch vs Community Watch

Since its inception, Neighborhood Watch has had varied degrees of success. Principally administered by law enforcement, successes and failures are generally attributed to the levels of commitment on the part of the people in charge of the program.

In many cases, when budget cuts affected the administrators' roles in the program, the program lost its driving force. Since many people in law enforcement are upwardly mobile, they tend to look for promotion and in many case a promotion moves an officer out of the unit to be replaced by an individual with no idea of how to run the program and they essentially start from scratch every year or two.

In Community Watch, the members of the community take responsibility and control of the program. A steering committee with rotating members sees to it that the program remains active even if volunteers rotate in and out of the program.

While Neighborhood Watch groups can and do exist in Community Watch programs, Community Watch programs generally do not exist in Neighborhood Watch organizations.

Another issue is when law enforcement administrators change in a jurisdiction, often their belief on non-belief in proactive programs will cause a law enforcement managed program to be terminated or altered to meet the needs of the law enforcement leader and not in the interest of the community.

If you think of a neighborhood, generally the image that comes to mind is a street with rows of houses on either side; whereas, if you think of a community, a more vague image of a group of people comes to mind. The term community can represent an apartment complex, a housing project, a business district, a church group or any number of groups that form almost every community.

It is not just a geographical difference either. The history of Neighborhood Watch is almost exclusively devoted to crime prevention, while a Community Watch can concern itself with any issue of importance to the people making up the group. It can include things like disaster preparedness, health and safety issues, civic planning issues, school integrity, or anything else that is important to the members of the community.

Operation ID

This program encourages citizens to mark their property with identifying numbers and maintain a registry of the numbers and marked items. The National Sheriff's Association has the most pervasive program at present.

RESULTS: Recovery of stolen property, deterrence of household burglaries, and prevention of other crimes of opportunity committed during break-ins. These crimes of opportunity include rape, murder, vandalism, auto theft, and assaults.

Business Watch

This program is similar in nature to Community Neighborhood Watch and involves individual businesses enacting training in crime and loss prevention. It also trains the businesses' staffs how to handle crime when it occurs. The other parts of the program involve businesses communicating to each other about suspicious activity, or criminal acts in progress. Businesses use a variety of communication methods, including: newsletters, fax machines, email, texting, and meetings for training and information sharing. The program includes loss prevention information on liability incidents, employee, vendor and customer theft, as well as other ways businesses are exposed to potential losses.

RESULTS: Reduction and prevention of shoplifting, employee theft, check fraud, assault, rape, vandalism, muggings, drug offenses, burglary, robbery, credit-card fraud, con games, and various other types of victimization.

Mobile Watch

In every community, every day there are assorted vehicles conducting a wide variety of tasks and missions. Almost every vehicle and driver has a phone or two-way radio. Valuable information can be relayed to the law enforcement or other safety organizations, if members of Mobile Watch System have been properly trained in spotting suspicious activities and potential dangerous situations, and the members are motivated to act when they see something. "Be on the look out" bulletins can be disseminated via fax, radio, text, and phone calls to advise them to assist law enforcement agencies to find abducted children and perpetrators in flight.

In some areas, HAM (amateur radio) operators patrol the streets alerting police to potential crimes in progress.

Busses, taxis, utility trucks or sales people can be trained how to report, respond to emergencies, how to report suspicious activities, and how to get and give accurate descriptions of cars and criminals.

RESULTS: Expedient reporting of burglaries, robberies, abductions, assaults, rape, drug offenses, plus gaining a timely description of suspects, getaway cars and direction of escape. Added gains are disaster preparedness, health, safety, and civic planning issues.

School Watch

Recent insolents of mass murders at our schools have prompted a serious look at how to protect our children. Short of having armed guards, police officers, or arming the teachers a solution is to have parents or other volunteers patrol the sidewalks in front of a school with a direct line to law enforcement to report any suspicious activity.

Similar to the other watch programs in principle, this program is a watch system set up to utilize the staff and students as both prevention and reactive information sources. (It should be noted that fire departments have made very good use of schools for years in fire prevention and reaction training programs.)

RESULTS: Reduction in crimes of violence, date rape, rape, abductions, murder, gun-related assaults, drug activities, gang activities and vandalism.

Drug and Substance Abuse Education

The problem of drugs has been with our society for as long as we have had a society. Some programs have been effective and others not so much. There is much more dialogue about the pleasure of using drugs than the problems associated with them, that the problem has been growing exponentially over the past few decades.

In order for a program to be effective over the long term, it needs to have a consistent message about why drugs are dangerous, an educational component for everyone in the community and a consistent effort to keep drugs off the street. The effort also needs to include alcohol, tobacco, and marijuana because research proves that if we can keep our kids away from these substances prior to their maturity, the odds of them becoming addicted is substantially less.

RESULTS: A population better educated about the dangers

associated with drug use, coupled with a consistent message from the media, and a strong interdiction component from law enforcement will in a reduction in demand, and availability of both legal and illegal drugs. Since the majority of crime is drug related, this will cause a substantial reduction in crime.

Campus Watch

Similar to school watch, this program focuses on the college campuses within a community. It addresses the specific needs of campus crime prevention with additional focus on violent crimes committed against young people.

RESULTS: Reduction in rape, robberies, assaults and other violent crimes directed at college students.

Community Watch

This program involves first training officers in how proactive and reactive methods work together. The second phase of this program is a "how to" system of "Beat (street) Management" which teaches the line officer the resources available to both prevent crime and react more decisively when a crime does occur. This is accomplished with a step-by-step system of community involvement. This program empowers the officers to use formal and informal resources to address the "crime problems" in their beat areas with a proactive — reactive plan of action.

Ideally, an officer would spend time, either walking a beat or participating in a meeting with community members to help the officer see the better side of the people he was hired to protect.

RESULTS: A more positive police image in public eyes, reduced crime of all types, and a quicker response and resolution to crimes that have already occurred.

CPTED

There is a significant body of research that proves crime prevention through environmental design, works. This part of the program involves the building community and regulatory bodies working together to enact standards consistent with known planning methods of crime prevention through environmental design. The concept of CPTED has to be interwoven throughout the entire Community Watch program. (It is important to note that for many years, communities have been regulating fire codes to protect lives and property. If communities were to enact codes for crime prevention, would this not also result in protecting lives and property?)

RESULTS: Reductions in all types of crime through passive measures.

Other Program Possibilities

The possibilities are endless but could include:

Disaster preparedness

A program to prepare people for potential disasters that can include evacuation measures, communications networks and emergency shelter organizations.

Citizens' Police Academies

A program to teach citizens about police procedures and how to work with the police agency to keep the streets safe.

Court Watch

A system to insure that the judicial system is working according to the wishes of the community.

Neighborhood Justice Centers

An alternative to the municipal or county justice system to make sure defendants are treated accordingly to the seriousness of the crime. This also removes much of the burden now experienced by the court system.

Managed Youth Centers

Providing a safe place for young people to go and find some positive role models and alternatives to current questionable activities.

Adjunct Programs

There currently exists a wide variety of programs which operate in various areas of the community as either a proactive or reactive effort to reduce crime and criminal activity. These programs need to be evaluated in terms of effectiveness and integrated into the Community Watch program, or be eliminated.

Some examples of these programs are:

1. Crime Stoppers

2. Mc Gruff

3. Child Safe

4. Battered women's shelters

5. Rape crisis centers

6. Victim/witness assistance programs

Education

The ability to identify areas of training needed to enhance the quality of life in a community will surface as particular challenges arise. The Community Watch program will enable communities of all sizes to address and correct any problems that may occur over time. The net result will be the improvement of the community's livability.

Chapter 8

How to Fix It

If you made it this far into the book, congratulations! Now it's time for the payoff. I hate watching the news because they just point out the problems without offering any solutions. We can improve the quality of life in all of our cities and towns. And, now I will show you how.

Initially, the crimes and other threats that affect us most have to be our main areas of focus. We need to begin training the town folks about how to take back our streets. In the 1990's I developed a complete library of videos to assist in the training of both law enforcement officials and residents so they could join with law enforcement to make our streets safe and help our kids stay drug free. Even though these training materials are available now, they do need to be updated to meet current expectations.

The first area of training would be to help people understand that they really can make a difference. People need to see what others have done in similar circumstances that actually made a change for the better. The EMMY-Nominated television program, _A Line In The Sand - Taking A Stand Against Crime_, demonstrates how people getting involved can save a life and lack of it could cost one. It also showed what involvement looked like and how with minimal time invested, one person could change the entire complexion of a community. This video has been used in countless neighborhood and Community Watch meetings. It has also been broadcast on live television in different parts of the country. It is currently available on YouTube on the Tom Monson Productions channel.

The first and most important place to eliminate crime, is in our homes. The video *Blueprint for Home Security* when incorporated with the Home Security Survey and Household Inventory helped people feel safe at home. In fifteen minutes, this stand-alone video teaches people how to make their homes safe. The two forms help them correctly go through the process of "Target Hardening" their homes and recording the items that are popular targets of theft.

Other topics of personal safety and violence prevention are also important issues for most people. Training in this area is also important to make people feel safe in their own skins wherever they may go.

Some of the most serious crime-based problems that exact the greatest amount of suffering are related to drug abuse. In many areas, estimates are that 80% of crime is drug related.

Why not leave it to the government? Current efforts by government agencies are best described in the way the budget is broken down. The areas of expenditures by task are as follows: Treatment (39%), Domestic Law Enforcement (33%), Interdiction (18%), International Efforts (5%), and Prevention (5%). A very wise man, Benjamin Franklin told us, "An ounce of prevention is worth a pound of cure." If you look at the percentages, our government has it exactly opposite (5% is 1/20th).

Possibly, if the people in our government, took the time to talk with people who were not lobbyists, special interests groups, or entrenched bureaucrats in the health or law enforcement agencies, maybe we could come up with actual solutions.

Over an eight year period, I produced 13 television shows that talked about all the aspects of drug and substance abuse. We aired these programs on television stations across the country with very positive results.

Estimates are that crimes against business costs the American consumer billions of dollars every year. These activities fund terrorist organizations, crime syndicates, drug addicts, and individual criminals. The problem continues to grow.

In some regions, these crimes are not even prosecuted. In 1990, I created a program called Stop Business Crime. It helped business owners understand the problem with crime and gave them inexpensive solutions to reduce the number of thefts.

Back then, I worked with The Chicago Police Department, In particular a Crime Prevention Officer named Rose Olivary. Rose told me one day she was showing this video to a group of managers for a major retailer and one of the managers slapped her forehead proclaiming, "I can't believe it! That's how they are doing it!" Rose told me that the department set up a sting and caught internal thieves who reportedly stole over $250,000 from this single store.

To respond to the training needs of business we have produced several programs to educate employers and employees to curb this type of crime.

In a response to a murder committed by two robbers looking to score some quick cash, we entered into a joint venture with Virginia Tech to create a training film to help retail clerks learn techniques to survive an armed robbery.

Additional Training Is Needed

The need for current training programs to address important issues will continue as long as there are important issues to address. There is a need to create training programs to empower both law enforcement and the people they serve.

Here are a list of topics with descriptions for training programs.

Crime-Free Multi-Housing Program

The concept of finding an effective way to keep apartment buildings and housing projects safe requires a consistent educational program to teach residents how to recognize suspicious activities and the motivation to report them. An effective program has the potential to reduce drug dealing, prostitution, robbery, rape, murders and crimes against children.

Drug and Substance Abuse Education for Teens and Preteens.

Drugs and substance abuse are killing teens more today than ever before. Even though there are many programs out there today, a community-wide effort on the part of all the people is the only way to keep those numbers at a minimum. It's not just up to law enforcement to protect our youngsters. It is the responsibility of everyone in the community to separate teens from drugs, alcohol, tobacco, and pot.

Workplace Violence Training

The need for training in the workplace is always present. Training needs to include, what to do when confronted by an armed robber, an active shooter, violent customers and coworkers. Each type of situation requires training for potential victims, victims, managers, and responders. This training should be part of the training one receives when they are hired and updated at least annually.

Personal Safety

Teaching personal safety to individuals will never go out of fashion. Muggings, murders, assaults and other crimes committed against individuals are on going and people need to know how to keep themselves and their loved ones educated and safe.

Sexual Assault Prevention

Over the past twenty years the chances of a woman being sexually assaulted have risen from one in five to one in three. Potential victims knowing how to avoid dangerous situations can greatly decrease this crime. This training could also include abduction for sex trafficking purposes.

Child Safety

Crimes against children are crimes against us all. Often children have no knowledge of how to protect themselves and stay safe. The responsibility of protecting our children is something that we must all take on. Programs need to focus on what each of us can do to keep our children safe. We must all commit to keep their future bright.

Disaster Preparation

People need to be trained on how to organize and prevent needless loss of life and property during or as a result of large-scale disasters. Recent floods, hurricanes, earthquakes, fires, chemical spills, and other potential community-wide disasters indicate a strong need for such a program. Prevention of looting and other criminal activities should also be a focus of training.

Robbery Prevention

Robberies most often happen when motivated criminals with the means and knowledge, find soft targets. A uniform and consistent training program will reduce the numbers of armed robberies. The evidence is clear that prevention works, yet these crimes continue to occur in record-breaking numbers. A standard training program should include the ideas and devices that are known to reduce these crimes.

Fraud and Con Prevention Education

Victims of these types of crimes are most often elderly and defenseless. Educating them how to protect their assets and their futures will not only help them, but also create less demand on social services and law enforcement.

Domestic Violence Intervention

One of the most dangerous calls a police officer responds to is domestic violence. Domestic violence occurs for a number of reasons and may require a number of resolutions. A program designed especially as a tool for law enforcement interdiction would offer needed help for those in need.

Why Hasn't This Been Tried Before?

It has. More than fifty years ago, numerous programs were started that effectively reduced crimes of all kinds. The results were mixed. The programs with the right management and motivation were successful. However, many of the programs set up without key ingredients failed.

This is paralleled in business. Of all new business start-ups, ninety-five percent of them fail within five years. The process of running an effective Community Watch organization is very similar to running a business. It will succeed for the same reasons a business will succeed, and it will fail for the same reason a business fails. Knowing and following management fundamentals are necessary for any organization to survive and prosper.

In a Community Watch program, it is not just an organization that loses. The crime and violence that are left to thrive in the absence of a working organization costs the people of the community dearly.

Fathers and mothers lose their dearly beloved children and people are violated in so many ways. Needless pain and suffering, lower quality of life, lost property values, business that goes somewhere else, and lost jobs are among the prices paid for a failed or inactive Community Watch.

Over the years, I've worked with hundreds of small business owners and taught them how to run a profitable businesses. Almost without exception, the people who succeed are the ones that follow a proven plan, like the one found in *Community Watch Administration*.

Chapter 9

Administration

In the past, crime prevention efforts have been primarily the function of local police departments and sheriffs' offices. Officers, volunteers, deputies, and employees have taken on the job of reducing and prevention crime in their given jurisdiction. Often these hard-working individuals are acting as practitioners (doers), trying to single-handedly stem the tide of crime. It is common for these individuals to work without the wholehearted support of their departments. They are often either token efforts (because of political reasons), or people put in the position as "rubber guns" (because they are perceived as being inadequate to participate in "real police work").

The position to oversee a Community Watch should be an administration-oriented individual whose primary function is to direct the total program. The goal of the program should be to enact a nuts-and-bolts plan of action that uses best practices in an integrated and coordinated effort.

The Community Watch Administrator must organize the group around a common goal to keep the members of the group engaged. The primary duty of the administrator is to bring all concerned into a common spirit, transcending the traditional turf boundaries of existing law enforcement agencies — to get everyone working together to make the community safe for everyone.

Even though many programs started with the leadership of law enforcement are successful, the vast majority of surviving and successful programs were started through law enforcement and then ownership was taken over by community members.

The best way to insure the success of a Community Watch program is to create a partnership with the community. (To repeat Sir Robert Peel: "The police are citizens and the citizens are police.")

Funding

The Community Watch plan calls for the reallocation of existing funds. These funds are currently being used for various programs which are not working effectively in their present applications. (The best evidence of this is the fact that generally, the crime rates across the board are continuing to rise.)

Citizens and businesses are often willing to help with the initial start-up expenses. If they don't already know it, they quickly understand that they already pay increased insurance rates, higher taxes, higher retail prices, and lose their possessions to the criminals.

Since the business community loses hundreds of billions of dollars to crime each year, a possible reallocation of these moneys could be funneled into Community Watch programs.

The average cost for a business to prosecute a single shoplifter is $3,000 - $5000 and through the criminal justice system the tax payers contribute an estimated one hundred fifty to two hundred billion dollars each year to prosecute the perpetrators. That's why both businesses and prosecutors are unwilling to prosecute low-level non violent crimes.

Even though a small initial up-front investment may be required, the overall long-term savings realized from a Community Watch program could be as much as $1,000 for every $1 invested. When you do a cost benefit analysis of a program, it becomes clear that Community Watch is a great investment, not even taking in the quality of life gained by the town folk.

Over the life of the program, these funds will be used to purchase training and materials for participants. Just like weeds in a garden, due to the nature of criminal activity, the need for this project will always be there.

Potential Funding Sources

1. **Banks**, through the Community Reinvestment Act and monies already allocated to robbery prevention.

2. **Insurance Companies**, reduce losses.

3. **Mortgage Companies and Brokers**, improve livability in property values.

4. **Real Estate Companies and Agents**, improve marketability of properties in market area.

5. **Home and Commercial Builders**, improve marketability of building projects in market area.

6. **Retail Businesses**, gain additional profits from less shrink and improved business caused by reductions in crime.

7. **Corporations:** improved livability for their employees and working environments.

8. **Security Companies** increase profits by increasing awareness and value of services.

9. **Homeowner's Associations** gain increased property values.

10. **Taxes** savings of investigations, prosecution, incarceration, and parole boards can be reallocated to the program.

11. **Phone and Cell Phone Companies,** additional profits are

gained by improving public relations and awareness of services, and improved livability for employees.

13 **Industrial Parks.** Improved property values, reduced security costs, and personal safety for employees.

14. **Manufacturers** safety of employees and increased profits from sales generated by increased public awareness of products.

14. **Public Utilities** gain by their community service and community relations efforts.

15. **Service Clubs** fulfill their missions and improve the quality of life in their service area.

16. **School Systems and Boards** provide a better environment for their staff and students.

Why Community Watch?

What I have to show you, is how to build an organization that will teach people to work with law enforcement to do several things:

1. Provide guaranteed reductions in crime. You can send a clear message that your community doesn't tolerate criminal activity. Let the criminals stay where they are — somewhere besides your community.

2. Make your community safe for all who live there. This means that people can walk down the street, attend school, go to the park, or just enjoy the freedom to come and go as they please without the fear of becoming a victim of a crime.

3. The positive action of putting neighbors back into neighborhoods. In other times and places, neighbors have looked after each other and each others' property.

Community Watch has proven to get neighbors together, not only to deal with the problems associated with the neighborhood, but to form lasting bonds as friends and people who care about each other.

4. Lower insurance rates. It's a very simple fact that where crime is lower so are insurance rates. Some insurance companies will offer discounts to people who have taken measures to prevent burglaries and other events. Based on individual areas, the more insurance companies pay out in claims, the more they charge in premiums.

5. Increased property values. If you were trying to sell two identical properties, one in a high crime area and the other in a crime-free area, which one would attract more buyers? And demand increases.

6. Lower taxes. If you reduce costs for law enforcement, detention facilities, courts, and the correctional system, you will cut taxes. If crime is reduced, the demand for law enforcement is also reduced. The limited space in our jails can be left for the worst offenders. We can keep the criminals where they belong, instead of letting them out to roam the streets.

7. Create better business conditions. This means more jobs for the people who live there and more money flowing into the community from increased commerce. All types of business will enjoy a better position because of the community's involvement in the program.

Does It Really Work?

When we released *Community Watch Administration*, First Edition, I personally visited twenty police departments and sheriffs' offices. Out of the twenty, nineteen told me that this program would benefit the people of their communities.

Subsequently the program was adopted by Camilla, Georgia, Wyoming, Ohio, and Jackson County Oregon.

Camilla, GA

A little town in southern Georgia became one of the first jurisdictions to introduce the Community Watch System.

After the initial set up of the program, Lt. Randy Shelton told us he had been trying to put the pieces of this puzzle together for over a year and had not been able to get their program off the ground.

Just before Thanksgiving last year I spoke with Lt. Shelton and asked him how it was going. He told me that the city had already reduced crime by about ten percent. I was surprised! I asked him if he was sure and asked him how he had recorded the rate. I also told him that it was very unlikely that his crime rate had gone down so quickly.

I explained to him that normally crimes like burglary, theft, assault, and rape go unreported. The reasons vary, but it is rare to have a true picture of a community's crime rate. When a Community Watch program begins, people start reporting crimes historically they would not have reported before.

All the newly reported crimes gives the appearance that the crime rate is increasing, when it is really presenting something closer to the true picture of the crime rate. After I explained all this to him, he still swore that the crime rate had actually gone down since the program's inception, and even more impressive, was that the people of his town were starting to regain a sense of community and were feeling safer than they had for years.

Wyoming, OH

The Chief of Police in this small town located on the outskirts of Cincinnati wanted to start a Community Watch Program. He ordered his training officer to take care of it.

The training officer had been our customer for a couple of years and knew about the program. He told the chief that he needed to spend some money to purchase the right tools to get the program started. The chief agreed.

When he received the manual, he was unable to find the time to start the program. Wanting to follow orders he reached out to a woman who had reported a crime earlier that year. She worked at home and agreed to take some time to set up the program. He gave her the manual and other material and let her have at it.

This woman had no law enforcement or management training and yet she was able to get the program up and running in a few months. As I remember, she was able to thwart a crime in progress because of the training in the manual. The chief and the town were so happy they bestowed her with a commendation when one of her members reported the suspicious activities of two individuals who turned out to be suspects in an armed robbery that had just occurred.

This is another good example of Community Watch at work. We tell people "All you have to do is want a safer place to live and be able to read, and *Community Watch Administration* will provide complete instructions on what to do and how to do it. Not only that, it will tell you how to keep it going.

In this case, a mother simply wanted to live in a town where she and her family would be safe. She had a big stake and believed she could make a difference.

Jackson County, OR

Attempts to get a citizen-mandated community policing program underway to address rising crime issues had been attempted by Sheriff C. W. Smith's office for many of years. Their program had been delayed by lack of time and financial resources.

When the Sheriff's Department utilized *Community Watch Administration*, the program was quickly initiated and the benefits to the community were realized immediately. According to Captain Bob Kennedy, "The program is the A-Z of what we needed to make this investment in our community."

Chapter 10

Getting Started

If you are ready to establish a Community Watch program in your community, here is what you have to do:

1. First and foremost, identify someone who will be able to initially lead the program. Initially, they will have to be involved with:

   1. Planning - set goals
   2. Communications - set up a communications program for the program
   3. Management - design a management structure for the program
   4. Volunteers - identity, recruit, and train volunteers
   5. Meetings - design, schedule, and attend meetings
   6. Programs - develop a series of educational programs discussed earlier:
      a. How to Conduct a Home Security Survey
      b. How to Report Suspicious Activity
      c. Operation ID
      d. Block Home/McGruff House Program
      e. Personal Safety
      f. Sexual Assault Prevention
      g. Children's Safety
      h. Fraud and Con Games
      i. Auto Theft Prevention
      j. Active Shooter
      k. Disaster Preparedness
      l. Homeland Security
      m. And more

14. Motivation - keep all participants on the program to perform their jobs and attract new members
    a. Plan and promote events
15. Develop forms and reports for the program
    a. Block Maps
    b. Member Profile
    c. Telephone Tree
    d. Suspicious Activity/Crime Report
    e. Sign Application
    f. Meeting Attendance
16. Promotion - keep awareness of the program high in the community
17. Publicity - deal effectively with the media and press
    a. Write press releases for each phase of development
18. Resource Development - keep the program supplied with necessary resources
19. Evaluation - be able to show that the program is working:
    1. Design and execute surveys
    2. Tabulate surveys
    3. Report results
20. Leadership Development - learn how to develop the skills of program participants
21. Identify, and recruit Steering Committee members - a steering committee is the backbone of a Community Watch program,
22. Surveying the Community - find out what kind of crime is really going on and what will keep your community interested and involved in the program
23. Addressing Other Community Concerns - make sure that the program is always working to continually improve the livability within the community

This can be a daunting task, but fortunately, we have done all the work. Everything in the forgoing list is covered, in detail, in *Community Watch Administration*. The book also provides you with the necessary tools and forms to empower your citizens to make their community a better place to live and work.

How Long Will It Take?

Unlike communities who use the trial and error method, your community can establish a program in a matter of months. The manual gives you the marching orders and the tools to make the most of your time.

It has taken us decades to get to the point of wanting to call in the military to protect our citizens. But if we can get an effective Community Watch program working, it won't take decades to take back our country.

In many jurisdictions positive results have been achieved in as little as one year and reductions of certain types of crime have been reduced by as much as eighty percent over a ten-year period. It will take time, but there can be positive results in short periods if people will work together.

Unless something is done, the only thing we can count on is the problem will continue to get worse.

What Is The Best First Step?

First, is to recognize there is a problem and best, is to make a commitment to take a stand. Commit necessary resources and energy to initiate a Community Watch program.

Recent estimates tell us that it costs about $200,000 to equip and staff a twenty-four hour patrol car. By diverting the same amount into a proactive program, the citizens would enjoy the dividend of safer streets and the perception that as a collective force, they were taking positive action to make their community a safer place in which to be.

Press Release:

LAW ENFORCEMENT AND COMMUNITIES JOIN FORCES TO FIGHT CRIME

Newly released, *Community Watch Administration*, 4th edition lays out a path for community members and law enforcement to come together with a common cause of making the community a better and safer place to live and work.

According to the publisher, Tom Monson, "This book is a must for any community that wants to work with law enforcement to make their community a better place to raise children, live and work."

The 550 page manual, now in its fourth edition, shows how to organize a program, get people working with the police in a positive way and get the police working with the the people in a positive way.

"This is truly the where the concept of community policing lives," Monson Said. "Since many police officers rarely deal with average, law-abiding citizens, they can lose touch. Community Watch is a proven way to get officers out of their cars to interact with normal people."

Community Watch can also provide law enforcement with valuable information when they are either investigating a crime or when they are in the process of apprehending a suspect.

Within a Community Watch program, citizens are more likely to give assistance and information to the officers. Community Watch also trains the citizens to observe for and report suspicious activity.

"We designed the manual so that you could put it into the hands of almost anyone who wants to make their community better. The manual gives enough information to start and maintain a Community Watch program. I believed there was a way to make our country a better place. But it has to be done community by community."

The manual is the result of two years of research conducted with hundreds of law enforcement agencies who had been able to reduce crime. Every section in the manual is based on a program that effectively reduced crime.

Since its very first release in early 1993, it has received acclaim from both law enforcement agencies and organizations involved with community policing and crime prevention.

"The need for such a comprehensive publication is long overdue, so I was delighted to discover the "*Community Watch Administration* Manual" containing all information needed to not only begin successful Community Watch programs, but to maintain these extremely effective programs as well." Carole Howell, Douglas County Sheriff's Department.

"The manual has been a great source of information. I would recommend it to anyone. The information I got in my crime prevention training was not nearly as complete. If you get any questions about the integrity of your company, or the content of your manual, you may tell them to call me." Michael Byrum, Desoto Police Department.

"Your manual has provided a wealth of information in an

organized, step-by-step, easy-to-read format for implementation of the program." Stephen Nihiser, Federal Protective Service.

"I believe that this manual is the best effort in this area that I have ever seen." Michael Petty, Kerville Police Department.

"Upon review, I found the *Community Watch Administration* Manual quite beneficial. Communities will easily be able to follow the guidelines and be able to set up successful programs." Jacqueline D. Aker, National Crime Prevention Council.

"The program materials you produce are first rate. They are clear, concise and technically excellent." H.R. Salmons, Western Crime & Loss Prevention Institute.

The manual is divided into twelve (more added since then) sections that cover every aspect of crime watch from setting it up, to what and how to teach people at the crime watch meetings.

Monson concluded, "As we designed the manual, we also designed other useful tools necessary for a successful program. We produced videos, forms, meeting notices, decals, signs, and two other important handbooks for participants. We designed a complete system for Community Watch."

If you would like more information about the *Community Watch Administration* Manual or any of the materials designed for setting up a program, www.crimeprevent.com

Chapter 11

Conclusion

For some time, we have known that proactive and community policing programs work. Unfortunately, some police administrators believe the choice is reactive or proactive and often leave it there.

For the most part, communities that have seen significant reductions in crime and communities that maintain minimum criminal activity are utilizing a partnership with members of the community with the common goal of having a better place to live and work. The principles of the partnerships are both proactive and reactive.

A significant downfall in community safety comes when elected officials believe change is the best way to get elected and eliminate effective programs in the name of change without regard to the effectiveness of the program.

Where law enforcement has a robust commitment to the community and where the community is actively involved in the program, politicians are much less likely to "fix something that is not broken."

But the best way to insure the longevity of a Community Watch program is to put it in the hands of the people of the community.

By applying this existing knowledge in a results-oriented, unified effort, we can truly take action against crime and enjoy the results.

For many years, my team researched proactive programs throughout the United States. We identified many successful ones and recorded how they did it in *Community Watch Administration* so others could duplicate their success in any size community, town, or city of any size or scale.

It has become painfully obvious that there are only two positions we can take as individuals when it comes to our crime problem. You can choose to be either part of the problem or part of the solution. There are no shades of gray—no middle ground. If YOU do nothing, then nothing gets done and many would argue that you are a part of the problem.

If you chose to do something about it, you will be part of the solution. The good news is it doesn't take much time or money. It does take a commitment to spend a little of your time — maybe a few hours a year — a little money, and a commitment.

The alternative? Well, you know because you are seeing it all the time even day.

When you started reading this book, you didn't think you could do anything about crime and the quality of life in your community. But now you do.

Next time you hear a report on the news or Internet about some horrendous crime, you will know there is something YOU can do about it.

Just think of the crimes you can prevent, the little children who are brutalized, the young women who are kidnapped and killed, or the older folks who are swindled out of their life savings. Your involvement could stop those crimes. You can make a difference.

If you have to go in large groups with your phone cameras, do it. Just do whatever you have do, to keep your city streets and schools safe. You can make a difference.

The fact of the matter is, as individuals we can not only reduce crime, the threat to our freedom, but we can also prepare ourselves for any potential disaster that may occur.

I've seen people with little in the way of resources but a lot of commitment keep a check on the growth of crime. In fact, outbreaks of home burglaries have been stopped cold by average citizens working closely with law enforcement.

We have to do something. Otherwise, this may very well be the once great nation that like so many others in history, crumbled from within.

If we don't do something about crime and livability in our communities, who will?